Disney's Year Book 2002

Disney's Year Book 2002

GROLIER BOOKS

Published by Grolier Books

Grolier Books is a division of Grolier Enterprises, Inc.

FERN L. MAMBERG   *Executive Editor*
S. J. VICTORIA VERNER   *U.K. Editor*
ELIZABETH A. DEBELLA   *Designer*
KATHERINE M. SIEPIETOSKI   *Production Manager*

ISBN: 0-7172-6562-5
ISSN: 0273-1274

Stories on pages 14-25, 34-45, 56-67, 78-89, and all Disney character illustrations copyright © 2002 Disney Enterprises, Inc.

Pages 14-25: Written by Catherine McCafferty; illustrated by Alvin S. White Studio; © Disney Enterprises, Inc. Based on the "Winnie the Pooh" works, by A.A. Milne and E.H. Shepard. Pages 34-45: Written by Barbara Bazaldua; illustrated by Alvin S. White Studio. Pages 56-67: Written by Victoria Saxon. Pages 78-89: Written by Liane Onish; illustrated by Alvin S. White Studio.

Illustration Credits and Acknowledgments

6: © Ian Jones/St. James Palace/Via Newsmakers. 7: © Toby Melville/Newsmakers; © Max Nash/AP/Wide World Photos. 8: © Henryk T. Kaiser/Transparencies, Inc.; © Harry Cabluck/AP/Wide World Photos. 9: © David J. Phillip/AP/Wide World Photos. 10: © Hans Reinhard/Bruce Coleman Inc. 11: Renee Lynn/Photo Researchers, Inc.; © Fritz Prenzel/Animals Animals; © Fritz Prenzel/Animals Animals. 12: © Hans Reinhard/Bruce Coleman Inc.; © Jane Burton/Bruce Coleman Inc. 13: © David Carter. 26: © E. & P. Bauer/Bruce Coleman Inc. 27: © Steve Maslowski/Photo Researchers, Inc.; Superstock. 28: © Fletcher & Baylis/Photo Researchers, Inc.; © Bob & Clara Calhoun/Bruce Coleman Inc. 29: © Wolfgang Bayer/Bruce Coleman Inc. 30: © Patti Murray/Animals Animals; © Johnny Johnson/Animals Animals. 31: © W. Gregory Brown/Animals Animals. 32-33: From *Make Cards!* copyright © 1992 by Kim Solga, used with permission of North Light Books, a division of F&W Publications, Inc. 46: © David Hall/Photo Researchers, Inc.; © Ted Levin/Animals Animals. 47: © Birgit Koch/Animals Animals. 48: © M. P. L. Fogden/Bruce Coleman Inc. 49: © Dotte Larsen/Bruce Coleman Inc.; © Hans Reinhard/Bruce Coleman Inc. 50: © Rod Plank/Photo Researchers, Inc.; © Skip Moody. 51: © Skip Moody; © Michael Lustbader/Photo Researchers, Inc. 52: © Craig Jones/Allsport. 53: © Richard Drew/AP/Wide World Photos; © Mike Fiala/Newsmakers. 54: © George Nikitin/AP/Wide World Photos; AP/Wide World Photos. 55: © Bill Aron/PhotoEdit. 68: © JPL/ NASA. 69: © JPL/NASA.; © NASA. 70-71: © NASA. 72-73: Artist, Natasha Lessnik Tibbott. 74: © Runk/Schoenberger/Grant Heilman Photography. 75: © Denny Eilers/Grant Heilman Photography; © Denny Eilers/Grant Heilman Photography; © Franke Keating/Photo Researchers, Inc. 76: © Jeffrey Greenberg/The Picture Cube, Inc.; © Denny Eilers/Grant Heilman Photography. 77: © J. D. Sloan/The Picture Cube, Inc. 90: © Wood River Gallery/PictureQuest. 91: Courtesy, The Cyber Telephone Museum. 92: Courtesy, The Cyber Telephone Museum; Property of AT&T Archives, reprinted with permission of AT&T. 93: © Laguna Design/Science Photo Library/Photo Researchers, Inc.; Courtesy, Nokia Inc.; © Tom Tracy/Photo Network. 94: BWP Media/Newsmakers; © Alastair Grant/AP/Wide World Photos.

Contents

Prince William Takes Time Off

Prince William left Eton in June 2000. Then he took a year off and had some great adventures before going to University.

Prince William is back at school. In September 2001, he entered the University of St. Andrews in Scotland, where he is studying History of Art.

But in the year before entering St. Andrews, Prince William did a lot of exciting things. He celebrated his 18th birthday on June 21, 2000. And he left Eton College, the famous public school, with three A levels—Geography, History of Art, and Biology.

Then, William took a "gap year." "I wanted to get out and see a bit of the world," he said. And he did!

6

❦ In Belize, in Central America, he took part in military exercises with the Welsh Guards.

❦ On an island in the Indian Ocean, off Africa, he worked on a programme to help ocean wildlife.

❦ In Chile, in South America, Prince William

Prince William at work in Chile, building a walkway for local villagers.

Prince William at an official function with his father, Prince Charles.

helped build wooden walkways in a small, poor village.

❦ In southern Africa, he learnt about saving wild animals.

Prince William had lots of adventures during his gap year. And he also helped many people who needed assistance.

7

U.S. President George W. Bush and his wife, Laura, moved into the White House in January 2001.

America's First Family

The White House has been the official home of the president of the United States and his family for more than 200 years. It's in Washington, D.C., the capital of

Jenna (right) and Barbara (bottom) are the daughters of Laura and George W. Bush. They are twins.

the United States. And in 2001, the new First Family moved into the White House.

George W. Bush is the 43rd president of the United States. He took office on January 20, 2001. Bush was the governor of Texas before he became president.

George W. Bush is following in his father's footsteps. His father, George Bush, was the 41st president! This is only the second time in American history that the son of a president has also become president.

Laura Welch Bush is the country's new First Lady. She married George W. Bush in 1977. Before that, she was a librarian and a teacher.

The Bushes have non-identical twin daughters, Barbara and Jenna. They were 19 when their dad took office as president. They are away at university. But they will be spending time at the White House during their holidays.

There are also two First Pets in the White House. Spot is an English springer spaniel. And Barney is a Scottish terrier.

PARROTS: Personality Plus

Parrots are the clowns of the bird world. And they can be very entertaining to watch. In the wild, they fly through the air in noisy flocks. Their loud calls can be heard miles away. And they scramble about like acrobats in the trees. As pets in homes, parrots are admired for their beauty and cleverness—including their ability to copy the sounds that we make.

10

There are about 300 different kinds of parrot. They live in warm places all over the world. They are most common in Central America and South America, southern Asia, and Australia and New Zealand.

There are hundreds of different kinds of parrot. Shown here are masked lovebirds (opposite page), a scarlet macaw (top), rainbow lorikeets (above), and a pink cockatoo (right).

Neat Feet

Parrots have unusual feet. Most birds have three toes pointing forwards and one toe pointing back. But parrots have two toes pointing in each direction. This gives them a good grip as they climb trees. And some parrots even use their feet to hold food.

This fancy footwork is pretty cool. But a parrot's unusual feet make the bird wobble comically when it walks on the ground.

Parrots in the wild include macaws and lorikeets. In pet shops, the ones you will see most often are parakeets, lovebirds, and cockatoos.

Many, although not all, parrots have brightly coloured feathers. But *all* parrots have powerful, sharply hooked beaks. In fact, their beaks are so strong that parrots often use them like a "third foot"—to pull themselves up tree trunks.

Parrots can even crack nuts with their powerful beaks.

What fascinates people most about parrots is that they can mimic, or copy, human speech. The African grey parrot is especially famous for its ability to "talk." Other kinds of parrot, including parakeets and cockatoos, can also be taught to repeat words.

Parakeets and lovebirds make great pets. But many other kinds of parrot are now rare in the wild. This is partly because the tropical forests where they live are being destroyed. It's also because many are captured and sold as pets.

People should not keep rare parrots as pets. These clever, beautiful birds should be allowed to live free in the wild.

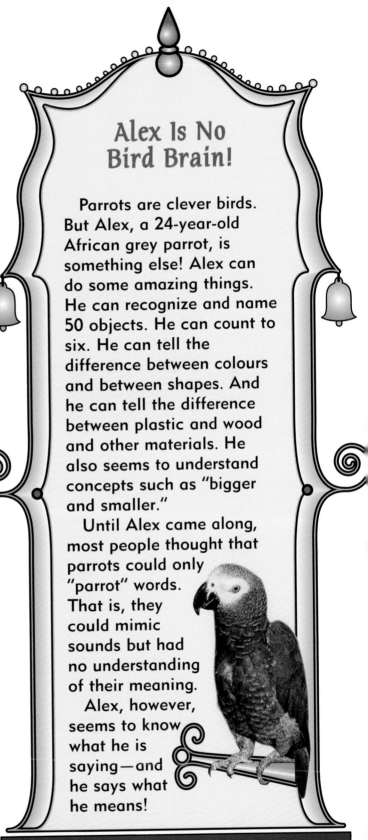

Alex Is No Bird Brain!

Parrots are clever birds. But Alex, a 24-year-old African grey parrot, is something else! Alex can do some amazing things. He can recognize and name 50 objects. He can count to six. He can tell the difference between colours and between shapes. And he can tell the difference between plastic and wood and other materials. He also seems to understand concepts such as "bigger and smaller."

Until Alex came along, most people thought that parrots could only "parrot" words. That is, they could mimic sounds but had no understanding of their meaning.

Alex, however, seems to know what he is saying—and he says what he means!

Kanga the Brave

Roo bounced out of bed, ready for adventure. Today, Roo decided, he would be Roo the Brave, Famous Explorer. He would find something really important in the deepest part of the Hundred-Acre Wood.

Roo the Brave hopped down the steps and swung open the front door. He was all set to dash out when his mother called, "Good morning, Roo, dear. Breakfast is ready."

"But, Mama," said Roo, "I'm going out for an explore. I don't have time for breakfast!"

Kanga just smiled and tapped the table. "A good breakfast will help you have a better explore," she said.

Roo the Brave frowned. Famous explorers shouldn't have to listen to their mothers, he thought. He dragged his feet all the way to the table, then started to gulp down his food.

"Don't gobble, Roo," said Kanga. "Take your time."

Roo tried to slow down, but he couldn't stop thinking about his explore. At last, he finished his porridge and drank his milk. He hopped off his chair and raced to the door.

"Where are you going, dear?" asked Kanga.

"Into the woods, Mama," he said. He puffed out his chest. "I'm Roo the Brave!"

"The woods?" said Kanga. "Dear, I don't think that's a good idea. Why don't we get the kite and—"

"Oh, Mama! Kites are for babies! I'm not a baby! I'm—"

"Roo the Brave." Kanga smiled. "I know. But you're still my little Roo, too. Now, put on your scarf, and let me pack a lunch. I'll come with you."

Roo wound his scarf around his neck. No famous explorer ever took his mother along on a dangerous explore! Especially not Roo the Brave! Before his mother had a chance to come back, Roo raced out of the door and into the woods.

"Tiiiiggggerrr! Tiiiiggggerrr!" Roo called. A moment later, Roo was bowled over by his bouncy friend.

"Say, Roo, what are you doing? Where's Mrs. Kanga?" Tigger put a hand above his eyes and looked around.

"Mama's letting me explore all by myself today," Roo said. He stood up as tall as he could. "I'm Roo the Brave, Famous Explorer. I'm going to find something really important in the deepest part of the woods." Roo thought for a minute. Every famous explorer had an explorer buddy. "Will you come with me, Tigger?" he asked.

"Hoo-hoo-hoo!" Tigger bounced around. "Tiggers love to explore. What are we looking for, anyway?"

"Something important. I'll know when we find it!" Roo said, hopping with excitement.

Roo and Tigger bounced deeper and deeper into the Hundred-Acre Wood, further and further away from their homes. At first, the sun helped light up the woods. But after a while, the sun went behind some clouds. The sky grew dark, and the woods grew darker.

"Say, Roo," Tigger said. "Have we come to that 'something important' yet?"

Roo looked around. "I don't know," he muttered. "What we're looking for is in the deepest part of the woods."

Tigger bounced a little way forwards, a little way to the left, then a little way to the right. "Yep, by my calckerlations, we're in the deepiest deep part."

Roo and Tigger stood still for a minute. The woods seemed very dark and quiet.

"I hope this isn't where the jagular hangs out," Tigger said.

BOOM! The sound made Roo and Tigger jump. FLASH! A bright bolt lit up the woods.

"Um, Tigger," Roo whispered, "I don't know if I want to find the jagular."

"Well, I think you found 'im, Roo boy, but we can outbounce 'im!" Tigger grabbed Roo's arm. They bounced off as fast as they could. But no matter which way they bounced, it seemed that the jagular was right behind them. Even to Roo the Brave, the thunder and lightning seemed like the growl of the jagular and the flash of his angry eyes.

"Tigger, I'm s-s-scared," Roo said.

They stopped bouncing and looked around. Rain was coming down so hard that they couldn't see where they were, or where they were going.

"It's a good thing tiggers never get lost," Roo said, looking up at Tigger hopefully.

"Er . . . tiggers need to see where they're goin' so they can't get losted." Tigger scratched his head.

Just then, another bright flash lit the forest. Roo and Tigger spotted a burrow under an old pine tree nearby.

"Let's wait under there," said Tigger. He pulled Roo into the burrow. Roo felt something yank on his scarf.

"The jagular's got me!" Roo yelped. He threw off his scarf and crawled as far into the burrow as he could.

"D-d-don't worry," Tigger said. "That big, old, fierce, scary jagular will never fit all the way under here . . . I hope."

The burrow was dry, but Tigger and Roo were soaked. Water dripped down Roo's face, but he didn't mind. The raindrops kept Tigger from seeing his teardrops.

The wind rattled the branches of the pine tree, and the thunder boomed all around them. Roo the Brave wished he were Roo the Home-in-Bed-With-Covers-Over-His-Head.

"I didn't even say goodbye to m-my mama," Roo said with a sniff. "And now I'll never see her again."

"Don't worry, Roo," said Tigger. "Once this rain stops, your ol' pal Tigger will get you home." With that, Tigger leant back against the side of the burrow and began to snore.

Roo leant back against Tigger, but he was afraid to close his eyes. Tigger's snores helped drown out the booming. Then Roo heard another sound.

"Oooooo! Ooooo!"

Roo nudged Tigger awake. "Tigger, I think the jagular is still after us!" he whispered.

"Persistent fella, isn't he?" said Tigger.

The sound came closer. Tigger and Roo crawled further into the burrow. Suddenly a light came towards them. Roo the Brave covered his eyes. He decided he didn't want to see a jagular, after all.

"Rooooo! There you are!" Kanga held up her lantern.

Roo peeked out. "Mama!" He jumped up and snuggled close to her. "How did you find us?"

Kanga pointed at Roo's scarf caught on a branch. "It's a good thing you took your scarf," she said with a smile.

Just then Roo heard an "Ooooo!" noise again. "The jagular!" Roo hid behind Kanga. Tigger hid behind Roo.

"It's all right, Roo," Kanga said. She stepped out and shook her lantern. "Go away, jagular!" she shouted.

There was a rush of wings, and then they heard a familiar voice. "I say, Roo," said Owl. "Did you find what you were looking for?"

Roo hugged his mother. "I did," he said. "I found Kanga the Brave, Famous Mama."

Baby Animals: Safe and Sound

As parents, apes rate A+! The world may be a scary place for this little one. But a hug from mum makes everything okay.

Baby animals face lots of dangers. A prowling cat might catch a baby bird. A fox may be hunting for a baby rabbit. How do animal parents protect their babies?

Sometimes a safe home is the best place for a baby animal. Baby animals won't be hurt if they are tucked away where enemies can't reach them. A mother squirrel builds her nest inside a hollow tree, high above the ground. Her babies grow up in their cosy nest. They are safe at home.

Even strong animals like lions make safe homes for their babies. When a lion mother goes hunting, she hides her cubs in a cave or a thicket. Sometimes she moves the cubs from one hiding place to another. She carries them one by one, by the scruff of the neck.

From baby squirrels to lion cubs, young animals need safe homes.

Hang on there! A baby monkey clings to its mum in the treetops.

Often the safest place for a baby animal is with its mother. If an enemy appears, mother and baby can escape together.

Baby monkeys are especially close to

A grebe carries her chicks on her back as she swims.

their mothers. A baby monkey clings to its mother's belly as she leaps from tree to tree. Baby monkeys know how to hang on tightly!

Grebes are duck-like birds that swim in lakes and ponds. They carry their chicks on their backs as they swim. Grebes are great divers. When a grebe spots an enemy, it quickly crash-dives. It disappears below the surface and swims underwater. And the little chicks go along for the ride, clinging to the parent bird's back.

When baby animals are in trouble, they often call their parents. When baby

For a baby crocodile, mum's mouth means safety!

crocodiles are scared, for example, they croak loudly. The mother crocodile hears them. She speedily comes sloshing through the swamp to help them. She may even open her huge mouth to take the babies in her toothy jaws! Then she carries them to safety.

Can you find this hen's chicks? Here's a hint: Count all the legs.

Some animal babies stay safe by hiding from their enemies. Young chickens are great at playing hide-and-seek. When chicks sense danger, they run to their mother. The mother hen fans out her wings and feathers, and the chicks scurry under her body. Now the mother looks like an extra-large chicken. You have to look very closely to see that the chicks are hiding underneath her.

Many other animal babies hide by blending in with their surroundings. In many cases, their colours help them stay hidden.

This lamb has found the perfect hiding place: Mum!

Baby deer, or fawns, can lie hidden in the woods for hours. A mother deer leaves her fawn in a woodland thicket. White spots on the fawn's brown coat blend with the pattern of sunlight coming through the leaves. The fawn lies perfectly still. It looks like a sun-speckled bump on the forest floor. An enemy may pass within a few feet and never know that the fawn is there.

White spots help a sleeping fawn look like a patch of forest floor.

It isn't easy growing up in the wild. But when animal parents protect their babies, they help make sure that the youngsters grow up safe and sound.

Paper Toys

You can have lots of fun making—and playing with—these paper toys. The perky pinwheel and silly snake start out as flat pieces of artwork. But with a few scissor snips, they will spin and dance!

Turn the finished pinwheel around with your hands until it moves easily. Then blow on it for a fast spin!

1. Cut a piece of paper into a 12-cm square. Draw an "X." Make four dots as shown.

2. Cut each of the four lines 6 cm in from the corners—not all the way to the middle. Poke a hole in the centre with a pushpin.

3. Decorate both sides of the paper. Draw a geometric design . . . or flowers . . . or animals.

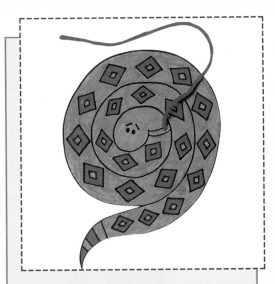

▲ Silly Snake

Draw a long snake all coiled up. Decorate both sides. Poke a hole near the snake's head. Tie on a long piece of string. Cut all the way up the spiral line and around the head. When the snake is cut out, it will hang in a spiral. Dangle it by its string and watch it dance!

4. Push the pushpin up through one of the corner dots. Bend the paper in so the pin is over the centre hole.

5. One by one, bend each paper corner, and push all the other dots up onto the pin. Don't prick yourself!

6. Push the pushpin through the centre hole of the pinwheel. Now poke it straight into the eraser of a pencil.

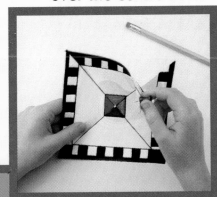

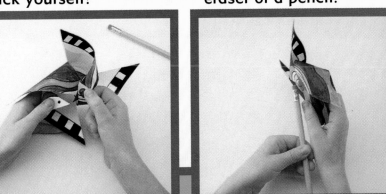

ALICE AND THE GIANT DORMOUSE

Alice sat at the tea party with the Mad Hatter and the March Hare, wishing someone would offer her something to eat and drink. It wasn't polite just to help herself without being asked. But she was so thirsty. "I'll just pour myself a small cup of tea," she muttered.

But as Alice began to pour the tea, a sleepy little Dormouse popped his head out of the teapot.

"Eeek!" shrieked Alice, who wasn't used to dormice—or any sort of mice—popping out of teapots. She dropped the teapot and watched it roll down the table, spinning the Dormouse until he was pink in the face.

As Alice lunged to catch the teapot, a small box fell from her apron pocket. On the outside were the words, "Eat Me," and inside the box were magical sweets.

It was the box she had found when she first fell into Wonderland! She had tucked it into her pocket before she shrank and fell into the pool of tears. But before she could put the box back into her pocket, the Mad Hatter grabbed it.

"What's this?" the Mad Hatter exclaimed. "'Eat Me!' Eat what?" He opened the box and found the tiny sweets. "Why, these look delicious," he said. He started to pop a sweet into his mouth.

"No! Don't eat it!" Alice cried. She knocked the sweet from the Mad Hatter's hand. It flew into the air and landed in the Dormouse's teapot.

For a moment, nothing happened. Then the teapot began to rumble and shake. It shattered into tiny pieces and out of it rose the sleepy Dormouse, who grew bigger and bigger with every second.

"Eeeeek!" screamed the Mad Hatter and the March Hare. They ducked under the table, which was starting to sag under the Dormouse's increasing weight.

"Aaah!" The Dormouse stretched, and the table broke in half.

"Help!" squealed the Mad Hatter and the March Hare. But the Dormouse just blinked and stumbled sleepily away, leaving footprints the size of fishponds in the Mad Hatter's flowerbeds.

Rubbing his eyes, the Dormouse crashed through the garden gate and wandered down the path. As he stumbled along, Alice could hear branches crashing and the birds shrieking as they watched his head go past their nests.

"I must stop the Dormouse before he smashes Wonderland to bits!" Alice exclaimed. She ran after him, but with his huge legs, the Dormouse was soon out of sight.

"Looking for someone?" A voice spoke above Alice's head. She looked up and saw the Cheshire Cat grinning at her from a branch.

"Do you know which way the Dormouse went?" Alice asked.

"Follow his trail," the Cheshire Cat answered. He pointed to a spot by the path where the bushes were as flat as pancakes. "He's taking little naps along the way."

"Thank you," Alice replied, and she ran on. She passed squashed shrubs, broken bushes, flattened flowers, and mangled mushrooms, but she still didn't find the Dormouse.

At last, she came to the Caterpillar, who sat smoking his pipe. "O, U again," the Caterpillar puffed when he saw Alice. "Y R U still here?"

"Have you seen a very large Dormouse come this way?" Alice asked.

"S Ndeed," the Caterpillar slowly replied. "E mangled the mushrooms. Find M N make M small again."

"U R right—er, you are right," Alice replied. "That's what I want to do, but I'm not sure how."

"Take some of that mushroom with you," the Caterpillar suggested. "I'd tell you which side makes you small, but I can't recall which is which."

"I'll just take a bit of both," Alice replied, breaking two chunks from the mushroom.

Suddenly she heard shrieks coming from the flower garden. When Alice raced into the garden, she found the Dormouse napping with his toes in the tulips.

"A monster is sleeping in our beds!" the flowers yelled. "He stamped on our stems and is pulling our petals!"

Alice knew that if she fed the Dormouse the shrinking piece of mushroom, he'd get small again. But if she fed

him the growing bit by mistake, he'd get even bigger. "Oh,
dear, what should I do?" she wondered.

"I'll have to test the mushroom pieces myself to find out
which is which," Alice decided. She nibbled a bit of mushroom
and—SWOOSH!—down she shrank, until she was no bigger
than a daisy. Now the Dormouse looked as big as a mountain.
And what was worse, just at that moment, he rolled over onto
Alice's other mushroom piece.

"Oh, dear!" Alice exclaimed. Now she was too small to reach
the Dormouse's mouth with the bit of shrinking mushroom.
And with him lying on the growing piece, she couldn't use that
one to get back to her real size.

Alice thought and thought. Perhaps she could wake him up.
She could ask him to move, or to nibble the shrinking piece of
mushroom, or, or—"I've got to do something!" she wailed.

Alice shouted at the Dormouse. She tugged at his fur. She even tickled his paws. But nothing woke him.

"Whistle loudly in his ear!" yelled the trumpet vines.

"Bite him on the knee!" growled a tiger lily.

"Stick thorns into him," the roses suggested.

Suddenly the Cheshire Cat appeared in the pansy bed. "Whisper the word 'cat' in his ear, my dear," he told her, just before he faded away.

"But how am I supposed to reach his ear?" Alice cried. "It's way up there, and I'm way down here!"

Just then a rocking-horse-fly fluttered by. Alice jumped on its back. Clutching the bit of shrinking mushroom in her hand, she flew up to the Dormouse's ear.

"Cat!" she whispered. "Cat, kitty, kitty, pussycat!"

"Caaaaaaaat!!" the Dormouse shrieked.

Quickly Alice threw the bit of mushroom into the Dormouse's open mouth.

SWOOSH! Instantly the Dormouse shrank to his normal size. Alice landed with a thump and scooped up the bit of mushroom that would make her grow. It was mashed—the Dormouse had been lying on it—but she didn't care. She nibbled and—SWOOSH!— Alice was her own size again.

The Dormouse was still running in circles, yelling about cats. Gently, Alice picked him up and popped him into her pocket. By the time she arrived back at the Mad Hatter's house, the Dormouse was dozing again. As the Mad Hatter and March Hare watched nervously, Alice tucked the dreaming Dormouse into a new teapot and put the lid on.

"He's himself again," Alice assured them. "But you really should watch what he eats."

And with that, Alice went off to find the White Rabbit. Maybe he would know how she could get home.

Living Together

Birds, trees, flowers, bees—there are millions of different kinds of animal and plant. They live everywhere in the world.

They live in places as different as a coral reef, a desert, an African plain, a rain forest, the icy polar regions, or a simple meadow. And in each place on Earth, animals and plants live together. In fact, they often depend on each other to survive.

▲ **Coral Reefs:** A coral reef is full of colour and life. Coral reefs form in warm ocean waters. They are made of the shells

of tiny animals called polyps. It takes lots of polyps, and many years, to build a reef. Seaweed grows on the reef. Colourful fish, crabs, and many other living things live and feed there.

▲ **Deserts:** Plants and animals need water, and there isn't much water in a hot desert. But some plants and animals manage very well. For example, a cactus can store water in its thick stem. Then the cactus provides food and water for insects and other animals. And desert birds come to eat the insects.

▲ **African Plains:** Zebras and giraffes live on the plains of Africa, where grass stretches for miles and miles. That means there is plenty to eat for plant-eaters like zebras and giraffes. The zebras in the picture above have come to a water hole to

drink. The giraffe seems to be standing guard. And there is good reason to be on guard. A lion could be on the prowl! Lions prey on other animals of the plains. At the first sign of danger, the zebras will run away.

▲ **Rain Forests:** Rain forests have more kinds of plant and animal than any other place on Earth! The forests have warm weather all year, and lots of rain, so plants just keep growing and growing. Trees and vines form a thick tangle. Insects, lizards, and snakes crawl among the plants. Birds fly through the treetops. Monkeys and other climbing animals make their homes in the trees. Larger animals, such as tigers and deer, live in some rain forests, too.

▲ **Polar Regions:** There is life even in the coldest places in the world. There are penguins in the Antarctic, polar bears in the Arctic, and lots of fish in both places. Polar bears and penguins will cross great sheets of ice in their hunt for fish.

▲ **Meadows:** In spring, a meadow is filled with flowers. Bees and other insects visit the flowers. They drink the nectar, a sweet liquid inside each flower. Spiders also live in meadows, spinning their webs among the flowers. If the insects aren't careful, they may be caught in a spider's web and become dinner!

All animals and plants have homes that suit their needs. That's why it's so important for people to protect wild places and everything that lives there.

A diamond-studded dragonfly? This sparkly insect looks like a piece of jewellery. But the dragonfly's jewels are drops of dew. The dew formed overnight, as the insect slept.

Which do you think is prettier, the red ladybird or the pink thistle? The ladybird spent the night on the thistle plant. Now both the plant and the insect are covered with glittery dew.

Dipped in Dew

Look at these glittery insects! They are covered with sparkles. They look as if they are going to a party! But those sparkles aren't sequins or jewels. The insects are covered with dew—tiny droplets of water. The dewdrops glitter in the first light of day.

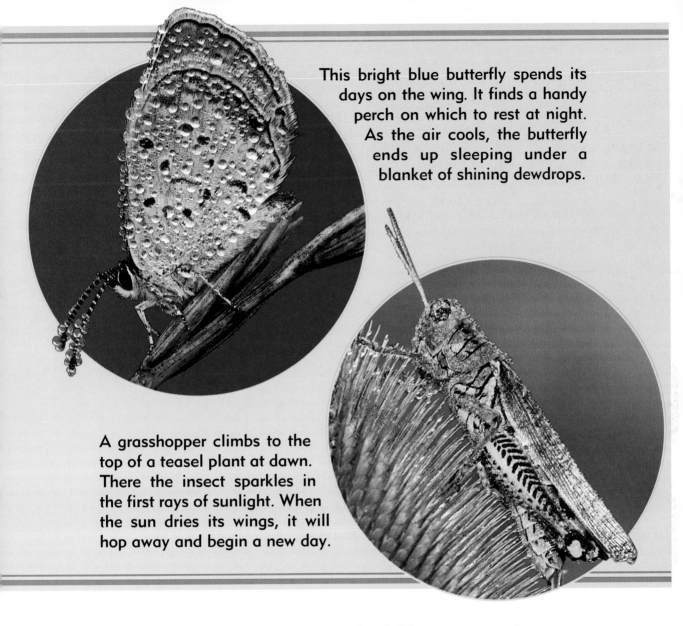

This bright blue butterfly spends its days on the wing. It finds a handy perch on which to rest at night. As the air cools, the butterfly ends up sleeping under a blanket of shining dewdrops.

A grasshopper climbs to the top of a teasel plant at dawn. There the insect sparkles in the first rays of sunlight. When the sun dries its wings, it will hop away and begin a new day.

Do you get up early in the morning? If so, you may have seen dew on the leaves and grass. Dew comes from moisture in the air. After the sun goes down, the air cools. Cool air can't hold so much moisture. So tiny drops of water form everywhere. Insects that spend the night outside end up sleeping under a blanket of dew. When the sun comes up, they sparkle and shine. But the sun quickly warms the air and dries up the dew. Soon the insects' wings are dry. They fly off and begin a new day.

51

Tiger Woods: Top Golfer

Tiger Woods is the best! His winning record in 2000 and 2001 proved that. This young man may even be the best player ever in the game of golf. One after another, Tiger won all four "majors"—the most important golf championships in the world. He became the first person to hold all four championship titles at once. And he was only 25 years old at the time!

Playing golf takes lots of skill. Players hit a tiny ball, trying to put it in a small hole hundreds of yards away. There are 18 holes in a game of golf. The

Another win for Tiger Woods— the world's top golfer.

player who finishes all 18 holes with the fewest strokes (hits) wins the game. And when Tiger Woods is in the game, he is often the winner.

Tiger's real name is Eldrick Woods. His father, Earl Woods, is a retired U.S. Army officer. Tiger's mother, Kultida Woods, was born in Thailand.

When Earl Woods was in the army, he had a good friend he nicknamed "Tiger." He nicknamed his son Tiger in honour of his friend.

Right from the start, Earl Woods steered his son towards the game of golf. He gave Tiger a little golf club and started to teach him the game almost as

. . . and so is Kultida, Tiger's mum.

53

soon as Tiger could walk! Tiger's parents helped him become a golf star. They are very proud of their son. And they have plenty of good reasons to be proud.

Tiger won his first golf tournament when he was only eight years old. Then he won many more championships, both in high school and at college. Then, in 1996, Tiger became a

Tiger Teaches

In 1997, Tiger Woods decided to help kids learn to play golf. Most of all, he wanted to help kids living in cities, who often don't have a chance to play. So he set up the Tiger Woods Foundation. The foundation raises money for junior golf programmes. And it holds clinics where kids get tips from Tiger himself!

TIGER WOODS FOUNDATION

professional golfer. As a professional, he would be able to play in big tournaments. And he would have a chance to win lots of prize money.

Tiger Woods won his first professional championship the very next year. And he hasn't stopped winning yet. He was named golf's Player of the Year in 1997. He was Player of the Year again in 1999. And he was Player of the Year for a third time in 2000!

Tiger's winning ways have been good for the game of golf. People enjoy watching him play. It is Tiger's love of golf that makes the game so exciting.

Lots of people have taken up golf after watching Tiger play and win. Many of those new players are youngsters. Bringing young people to the game is something Tiger thinks is very important.

Years ago, Tiger set a goal for himself. He said: "I want to be the best golfer in the world." Most people think he has reached his goal. Everyone expects that he'll be playing golf, and winning, for many years to come.

Milo's Rescue Mission

"Milo, come quickly!" cried Nabi, a cute 3,000-year-old girl from Atlantis, the ancient city beneath the ocean. She had been close to Milo Thatch ever since he had decided to live in the lost empire.

"Nabi, what's wrong?" Milo asked.

"It's Buke! He's gone!" Nabi said. Milo knew Nabi's brother, Buke, well.

"When did you last see him?" Milo asked.

"Yesterday afternoon," Nabi managed to say. "Some kids were teasing him, and—"

"Teasing him?" asked Milo. "About what?"

"About being small and—and—"

"And clever?" Milo added gently.

"Yeah," Nabi replied, her light green eyes peering up at Milo. Nabi knew that Milo had also been teased when he was a child. "Buke took my father's spear and mask. And he left a note saying he was going to catch a perkah gewarag!"

Milo cringed at the thought. The perkah gewarag was a giant cave-dwelling beast. It was one of the largest and most dangerous animals in all of Atlantis. Lots of Atlantean kids dreamed about catching a cave beast, but most were too scared to try.

"C'mon, Nabi," Milo said. "Let's go and see Queen Kida. Maybe she can help us."

The queen was in her royal chambers when Milo and Nabi arrived and asked permission to see her. It was dark and cool in the area where they waited. Deep pools of blue water were surrounded by lush green plants and old, mossy statues decorated with ancient Atlantean lettering.

"Milo?" Queen Kida stood in the doorway. She was dressed in a long blue robe, her turquoise tattoos glowing on her cheeks. A look of concern crossed her face. "What's wrong?"

"It's Buke," Milo answered. "He's missing. Nabi says he went out to hunt a cave beast yesterday afternoon."

"Then we must find him quickly. Give me a moment to change," Kida said. "I'll meet you by my Ketak."

"Of course," Milo replied. "C'mon, Nabi."

Milo and Nabi raced outside to a grotto where the royal vehicles were kept.

Instead of cars and lorries, Atlanteans used flying fish made of stone. The Ketak was Kida's speeder.

Soon Kida appeared, carrying her Atlantean shield and spear.

"Uh, your majesty," Milo said, "would you mind driving us so that I can look at the map? Maybe I can work out where Buke went."

Kida smiled. "You know I love to drive, Milo Thatch."

Soon Milo, Kida, and Nabi were speeding over the bustling city of Atlantis. Milo scanned his map.

"Nabi, did Buke tell you anything about where he was going?" Milo asked.

"Sort of," Nabi said. "Our father used to tell us stories about the caves near the city. Buke was scared, but he was curious, too. He used to go as close as he dared. Then he would watch the caves from behind a small ridge."

"Did he tell you anything about the ridge?" Milo asked. "Anything at all?"

"He said there was a kind of peep-hole formed by some of the rocks. He thought that when he looked through the hole, the cave beasts couldn't see him."

Milo remembered that he'd seen a place like that once. He looked at the map more closely.

"Kida!" Milo said suddenly. "I think I know where Buke is!" Milo guided Kida to the right, and soon she slowed the speeder and came to a stop.

"We should walk from here," she said quietly. "The cave beasts may hear the Ketak if we get any closer."

Milo pointed to a rocky hill. "My guess is that Buke climbed that hill and hid behind the rocks at the top to watch the entrance to the cave. The map shows that the cave isn't far beyond the ridge."

"Then that's our destination," said Kida. And with Nabi in the lead, they crawled up to the ridge.

"Nabi, does this look like the place Buke described?" Milo asked.

"Oh, yes!" Nabi whispered back. "It even has a place to peek out at the caves!"

"Good," Milo said. "I think we're close."

But Milo had a sinking feeling. They *were* close, but there was no sign of Buke. Now what should they do? Where could he be?

"I'll go ahead," Kida said. "I might be able to track Buke by his footprints."

"I'm going with you," Milo said. "Nabi, you wait with the Ketak."

Nabi didn't answer. Milo turned around and saw her pointing down the rocky slope, her face pale. Lying on the rock below was the Atlantean spear that Buke had taken.

"Nabi," Kida whispered, "run back to the Ketak. If you think we're in trouble, return to the city and get help!"

"Okay," Nabi said. She turned and rushed down the hill.

After she saw that Nabi was safely away, Kida sprang over the rocks and scrambled down the slope. Milo followed her. At the bottom of the slope, they came to a group of boulders. Kida and Milo made their way cautiously around them.

And that's where they found Buke. His ankle was wedged between two rocks. He had fallen from the ridge and was stuck, but unhurt.

"Queen Kida!" he cried.

"Shhh!" Kida said softly. "The cave beast is near."

Swiftly, Kida pushed one of the boulders away, and Milo gently pulled the boy's ankle loose.

"Come on!" said Kida. "Let's get out of here before that cave beast changes his mind."

"What cave beast?" Milo asked.

"The one just inside that cave," Kida said, pointing to it. "He's been watching us for the past five minutes."

Milo looked in the cave. Sure enough, he could just make out two glowing eyes just inside the cave's mouth.

"Holy smoke!" Milo said.

"I guess we're lucky he's not hungry!" Kida said.

Helping Buke, Milo and Kida quickly made their way back to the Ketak and Nabi. Then they all climbed aboard the flying fish and headed home.

On the way, Buke thanked the queen—and Milo.

"Just promise me you'll never go out like that again," said Kida. "We could have lost you for ever."

"I know," Buke replied. "I'm sorry. I just wanted to be a hero so the other kids would stop making fun of me."

Kida parked her Ketak in the grotto outside the palace. "Buke," she said gently, "you don't have to battle a dangerous cave beast to prove that you are brave. In fact, the most courageous person I have ever met is a cartographer and a linguist."

"Huh?" said Buke.

"He studies maps and understands strange languages," Kida explained. "He used to be teased just like you. But he also saved all Atlantis from being destroyed. His name is Milo Thatch. And we would never have found you today without him."

MARS:
"The Red Planet"

What is the planet Mars like? This drawing shows a spacecraft landing on the planet's reddish, rocky surface.

Mars is Earth's next-door neighbour in the solar system. It is the fourth planet from the sun, and Earth is the third. People have always been curious about Mars. And now they are getting answers to some of their questions. Scientists are even close to answering the biggest question of all: Was there ever life on Mars?

People began to learn more about Mars as far back as 1976. That's when two *Viking* spacecraft landed on the planet and sent back pictures and information. There were no astronauts on the *Viking* craft, and people still haven't walked on Mars. But other spacecraft have visited the planet since then.

Mars Global Surveyor has been orbiting Mars since 1997. It mapped the planet's entire surface. Also in 1997, *Mars Pathfinder* landed on the planet and sent back live pictures. Then in April 2001, a new spacecraft—*Mars Odyssey*—began its three-year mission to observe and study the planet.

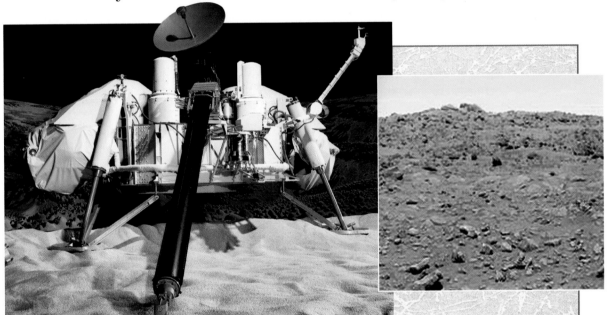

The First Mars Missions

The first spacecraft to visit Mars were *Viking 1* and *Viking 2*. The United States launched them in 1975. They reached Mars ten months later, in 1976. Then each craft released a small robot probe that landed on the planet (above left). The year 2001 marked the 25th anniversary of their amazing landings.

The *Viking* probes were packed with cameras and scientific instruments. They sent lots of information back to Earth. They analysed the planet's soil and air. They measured temperatures. And they took the first close-up pictures of the surface of Mars (right). The pictures showed a reddish desert filled with rocks. The reddish colour comes from minerals in the soil. That's why Mars is called "The Red Planet."

Here are some of the things these spacecraft have told us:

• **The Pear Planet:** Mars is slightly pear-shaped. Its southern half bulges out more than its northern half.

• **A Huge Hole:** Mars has an enormous crater. It is wide enough to stretch all the way from London to the north coast of Africa. And it is easily deep enough to hold Mount Everest, our world's highest mountain! Scientists think the crater was formed by an asteroid—a huge space rock—that crashed into Mars early in the planet's history.

• **A Martian Ocean:** Scientists think that Mars once had lots of water. There is a big flat basin in the north that may once have been an ocean.

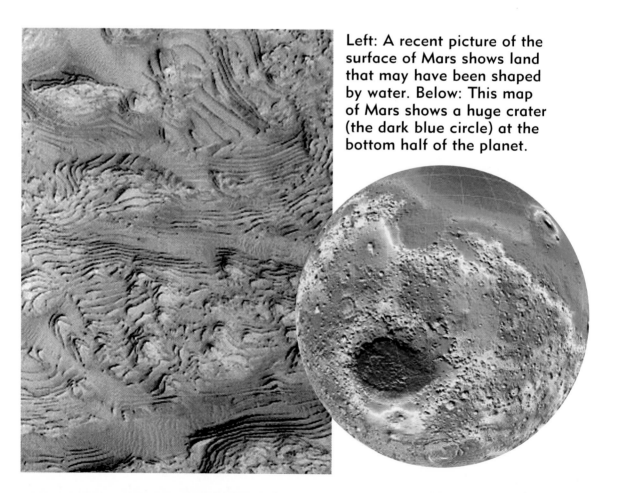

Left: A recent picture of the surface of Mars shows land that may have been shaped by water. Below: This map of Mars shows a huge crater (the dark blue circle) at the bottom half of the planet.

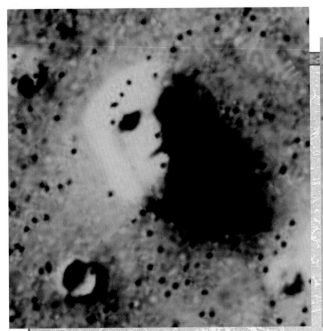
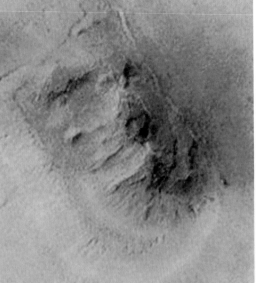

Now you see it . . .   . . . now you don't!

A Face on Mars?

The picture on the left was taken in 1976 by *Viking 1*. It seems to show a face staring up from the surface of Mars! Some people who saw this photo thought it *was* a face. And they thought it was created by an ancient Martian civilization!

Scientists didn't think so. In 1998, they made *Mars Global Surveyor* take sharper close-up pictures of the area. Those pictures, like the one on the right, show that the "face" is nothing but an ordinary hill with lots of bumps and dips.

Scientists have long believed that all the water on Mars dried up ages ago. Now they aren't so sure. Photographs taken by *Mars Global Surveyor* show land that seems to have been recently shaped by flowing water.

The idea of water on Mars is exciting. Life as we know it depends on water. So if Mars has water, maybe life could have developed there.

PASTA

You can make these clever pictures. All you need is coloured paper, white glue, and lots of pasta—stars, wheels, bow ties, shells, circles, spirals, and long, straight spaghetti!

First, decide on a design for your picture.

PICTURES

Here are some ideas: a butterfly, flowers, a heart, a train, a little girl.

Arrange the pasta shapes on the coloured paper. Glue the pasta—one piece at a time—onto the paper. Let it dry.

Remember, your pretty picture is great to look at—but not to eat!

Blowing in the Wind

What will the weather be like? Will it rain this afternoon? Will the sun shine tomorrow? It's easy enough to find out. All you have to do is turn on the television or the radio and listen to the daily weather forecast.

But 100 years ago, it wasn't so easy. No one had a TV or a radio. And there were no daily weather forecasts.

Which way is the wind blowing? The arrow of this weather vane points between "S" and "W"—so the wind is from the southwest.

Instead, farmers, sailors, and other people made their own forecasts. And one of the tools they used was the weather vane.

A weather vane shows which way the wind is blowing. That helps because certain kinds of

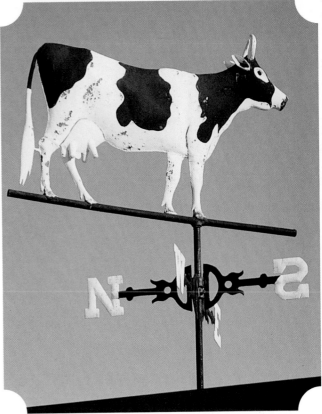

A golden turkey . . . a prancing horse . . . a black and white cow. Lots of weather vanes feature animals, especially in the countryside.

Above: When the wind blows, the farmer lifts the pump handle on this funny weather vane. Left: Does this old-fashioned bicycle weather vane look as if it's going to ride away?

weather tend to come along with winds from certain directions. An old rhyme says it best:

> A *wind from the west*
> *Brings weather at its best;*
> A *wind from the east*
> *Brings rain to man and beast.*

Weather vanes are usually placed on rooftops, where they catch every breeze. Up there, weather vanes are easy to see.

76

Old-fashioned weather vanes often showed favourite animals—cows, cockerels, fish, birds. Some were funny, and some were symbolic. The weather vane used by George Washington on his home in Virginia showed a dove. It carried an olive branch as a sign of peace.

This lobster weather vane sits on the roof of a business in a city. Can you guess what kind of business it is? A seafood restaurant!

Other weather vanes were used as signs for shops and businesses. By looking at the weather vane, a person could tell what kind of shop or business was inside.

Today we don't need weather vanes to work out the weather. But we still like to see them blowing in the wind!

Where There's a Well, There's a Way

Once upon a time, a sort-of-happy king and a sort-of-happy queen sat on the balcony of their castle, eating cake. Now, as everyone knows, a king and queen can't be more than sort-of-happy if their kingdom contains giants, dragons, ogres, or trolls. (They are, however, expected to eat cake every single day.)

The royal giant expert had just reported that the kingdom's giant was sleeping, and would—maybe, probably, hopefully—not wake for months.

"Mmm! What delicious cake, my dear," said the sort-of-happy king. Then, looking out on their kingdom, he added, "The farmers are in their fields. The townspeople are in their towns. The children are in their schools, and our daughter, Princess Daisy, is in the courtyard having tea and cake with Prince Seeya." Suddenly, however, the prince stood up and stalked off. He didn't even finish his cake!

"Our Daisy *was* having tea and cake with Prince Seeya. It looks as if Prince Seeya just said 'See ya!'"

The queen sighed. "Will she ever find a prince to marry?"

The king sighed, too. "Daisy is very particular. The prince must be brave, modest, honest, handsome, and able to rid the kingdom of giants, dragons, ogres, or trolls, as needed. And he must like cake. All or nothing for our Daisy," the king added. "None of the princes have it all."

"Then there is only one thing to do," said the queen.

With trumpets blaring, court officials posted the queen's notice. When the school bell rang, Huey, Dewey, and Louie rushed into the square to read the latest news from the castle. Here is what the queen's message said.

Hear ye, hear ye! The king and queen cordially invite any and all to rid our kingdom of the giant. The brave giant-ridder will marry Princess Daisy and live in the palace. He will also get to eat cake every single day!

The three boys rushed around the corner to their uncle's well-digging business. Now, this well-digging business was a poor well-digging business, and Donald and his nephews lived together in a few small rooms over the store. There wasn't much money, there wasn't much food, and there was no cake at all.

"Unca Donald! Unca Donald!" Huey cried. "You can marry Princess Daisy!"

"And we can all live in the castle! And eat cake every single day!" added Louie.

"Waaak!" cried Donald, waking from a dream in which he and Princess Daisy were holding hands. "What? Marry Princess Daisy?" His heart beat faster. "Why would she want a poor well-digger like me?" he sighed.

The boys dragged their uncle to the town square. Donald read the notice. "I'm no giant-ridder," he muttered. "Too bad. It would be nice to marry Princess Daisy."

Sadly, the nephews
followed Donald back home.

Waiting for them was Sir Horace, the
manager of the king's royal farms. "You, sir, shall have the
honour of digging the well for his majesty's newest farm," he
informed Donald.

Donald looked at Sir Horace's map. He pointed to a cave just
beyond the new farm. "Th-tha-that's where the giant sleeps!"
he squawked.

Sir Horace said, "Yes, well—the royal giant expert says that
the giant is sleeping, and will—maybe, probably, hopefully—not
wake for months."

"Ah, yes, well, um, er—oh, well," said Donald.

"We'll do it!" said Huey.

"We'll start right now!" said Dewey.

Donald was not happy working so close to the giant's cave, no matter what the royal giant expert said, but he and his nephews needed the money. Donald got their canteens, wrapped up a few crusts of bread, and he and the boys headed off to the king's newest farm.

Soon they began to dig. And dig. And dig. "Well-digging is no piece of cake!" Donald complained. Several hours later, he said, "Time for a break, boys." They stopped for a drink of water and ate a few crusts of bread. Donald and the boys wished they had some cake.

Then Donald said, "I'm going to nap. You can play, but don't go near the giant's cave."

The nephews began a
game of kick ball. Huey kicked
the ball to Dewey. Dewey kicked the
ball to Louie. Louie kicked the ball right into the giant's cave.

"Do you think the ball might—" said Louie.

"ARRRGH!" bellowed the waking giant.

"—wake the giant?" finished Louie with a gulp.

"Waaak!" cried the waking Donald.

"Now you can get rid of the giant, Unca Donald!" cried Huey.

"Are you kidding?!" squawked Donald. "Run!"

Donald and the boys ran every which way. Then Donald
tripped. "Yeow!" he yelped. The giant turned . . . and headed
straight for Donald!

Donald ran faster. The giant got closer. Suddenly, the giant fell—CRASH!—at Donald's feet. The whole countryside shook. Then all was silent.

"The giant's toe is stuck in the well!" said Dewey.

"The giant hit his head on that big rock!" said Louie.

"The giant has . . . vanished?!" cried Huey, Dewey, and Louie. They all stood and stared. The giant was no longer there. All that remained was a big dent the giant's body had made in the dirt. Then, looking up, Huey said, "Here comes Sir Horace!"

Dewey said, "And the king and queen!"

Louie said, "And the royal giant expert."

"And the beautiful Princess Daisy!" said Donald softly, his lovesick heart beating madly.

The royal giant expert circled the outline of the giant. "Yes. He's gone," he announced.

The boys were eager to tell the story. "Unca Donald got rid of the giant! He led the giant right to the well. Then the giant got his toe stuck and fell. The giant hit his head right here on this big rock and . . . disappeared!"

"What a brave giant-ridder!" said the happy king (no longer just sort-of-happy).

Donald blushed. "Oh, well, I, um, er—" he sputtered.

"What a modest giant-ridder," said the happy queen (no longer just sort-of-happy).

"Oh, well . . . you see, it was really an accident," Donald explained.

"What a brave, modest, and honest giant-ridder," said Princess Daisy, batting her eyelashes. "But where is the giant?"

Then, like magic (for it *was* magic), Daisy's fairy duck-mother appeared. "Fairy duck-mother!" cried Daisy. "What happened to the giant?"

"The giant wasn't a real giant," said the fairy duck-mother. "He was a test to find the most brave, modest, and honest man for you, my dear. This handsome fellow has proved his worth, so we have no more need for a giant. Still, there is one small detail we need to know."

Donald swallowed. "Yes, your fairyness?"

"Do you like cake?" she asked.

"He loves cake!" shouted Donald's nephews.

"And Princess Daisy," Donald whispered.

Donald and Princess Daisy were soon married. Huey, Dewey, and Louie moved into the castle with their uncle, now Sir Donald, and their new aunt, Princess Daisy.

And they all ate cake every single day.

Here is Alexander Graham Bell, showing how his telephone works. Nowadays we take telephones for granted. But in the 1870's people were amazed by Bell's telephone. They could not believe that the sound of a voice could travel over wires! Instead of "Hello," Bell liked to shout "Ahoy!" as a telephone greeting.

The Fabulous Phone

The telephone rings. Is it a call for you? The phone plays a big part in our lives. It helps us keep in touch with friends and family members. We can talk to people who are thousands of miles away. On the phone, they seem to be just next door!

What would life be like without phones? It's hard to imagine. Luckily, telephones have been around for a long time. In fact, the year 2001 marked the 125th "birthday" of the telephone.

The telephone was invented in 1876 by Alexander Graham Bell. Bell was born in Scotland but he moved to Canada when he was 23. He was a speech teacher who worked with deaf people.

The First Phone Call

This is Bell's first telephone transmitter—the part of the telephone that sends signals. On March 10, 1876, Bell was working in his lab with this device. His assistant, Watson, was in another room. When Bell accidentally spilled some acid, he called out, "Mr. Watson, come here. I want you!" Amazingly, Watson heard Bell clearly over a receiver that was wired to the transmitter. That was the first telephone call!

In Bell's day, the telegraph was the fastest way to send messages over long distances. The telegraph used electricity to send coded messages over wires.

Bell was fascinated by the telegraph. And he was sure that he could find a way to send speech, not just code, over wires. He hired an assistant, Thomas Watson. They set up a lab in a boarding house in Boston, Massachusetts. There, the two inventors went to work.

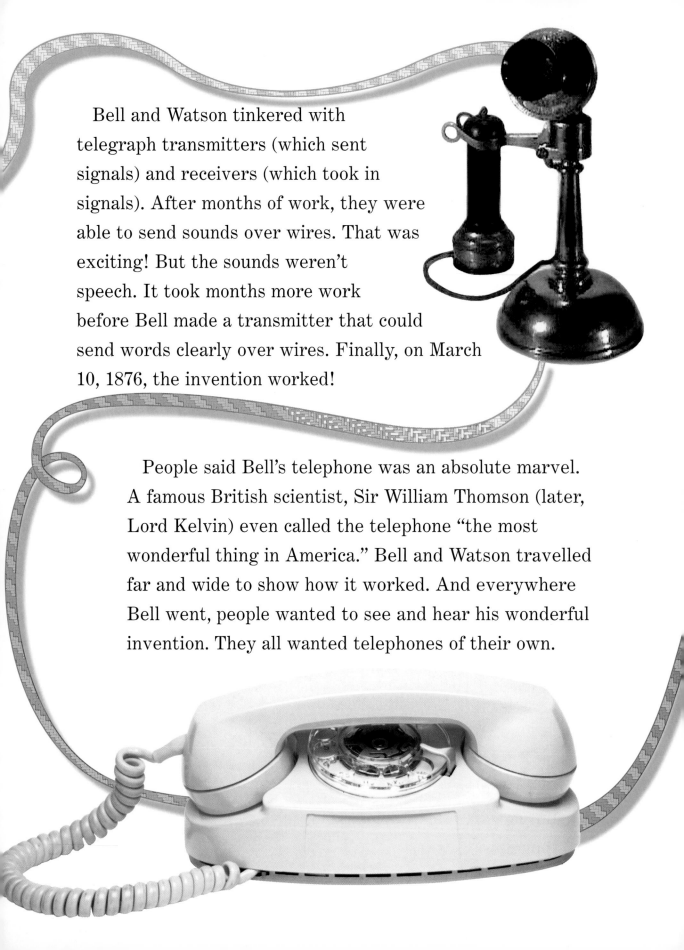

Bell and Watson tinkered with telegraph transmitters (which sent signals) and receivers (which took in signals). After months of work, they were able to send sounds over wires. That was exciting! But the sounds weren't speech. It took months more work before Bell made a transmitter that could send words clearly over wires. Finally, on March 10, 1876, the invention worked!

People said Bell's telephone was an absolute marvel. A famous British scientist, Sir William Thomson (later, Lord Kelvin) even called the telephone "the most wonderful thing in America." Bell and Watson travelled far and wide to show how it worked. And everywhere Bell went, people wanted to see and hear his wonderful invention. They all wanted telephones of their own.

Bell helped form a company to make and sell telephones. Soon thousands of people had phones. Long-distance lines linked big cities in the United States. Then telephone networks spread around the world.

Today we have all kinds of telephones. There are cordless phones, mobile phones, video phones, and even Mickey Mouse phones! And it all started with Alexander Graham Bell.

Bell was still a young man when he invented his wonderful telephone. He worked on many other inventions later in his life. But none of those later inventions was more important than the telephone. Alexander Graham Bell died in 1922. After his death, all the telephones in North America were silent for one hour in his honour.

Imagine coming face to face with this huge dinosaur! You can, at London's Natural History Museum.

IT'S A ROBODINO!

Dinosaurs roamed the Earth millions of years ago. Now one of the scariest of these giant reptiles is back! And you can walk right up to it at the Dinosaur Gallery in the Natural History Museum in London.

With its giant saw-edged teeth, this fearsome dinosaur looks like a *Tyrannosaurus rex*. It moves like a *T. rex*. It roars like one. It even smells like one.

But this *T. rex* isn't real. And it wasn't built from fossil bones. It's a giant robot that was built by a team of Japanese robotics engineers.

Robot *T. rex* is about 6 metres long—or about half the length of a real *T. rex*. It's controlled by a computer. When it senses you coming, it will stare at you with cold eyes, curl its lip or thrash about, and let out a terrifying dino roar.

Robot *T. rex* will even breathe its foul-smelling breath on you. Of course, its breath isn't real, either. It's just a special smelly oil, called "dragon's breath".

Would you like to visit this incredible robodino? It's the most fearsome robot *T. rex* in the world!

THE LIZARD KING!

◄ The name *Tyrannosaurus rex* means "tyrant lizard king." A tyrant is a strong, cruel ruler. *T. rex* wasn't a king— dinosaurs didn't have kings. But it was one of the most powerful animals of its day.

◄ *T. rex* was one of the biggest meat-eating dinosaurs. It was about 12 metres long and weighed 7 tons. It walked on huge, powerful hind legs. But its front legs were small and almost useless. *T. rex* snapped up its prey with its huge jaws and sharp teeth.

◄ *T. rex* had bumpy skin, like an alligator. But nobody knows what colour it was.

◄ *T. rex* walked the Earth 85 to 65 million years ago—long before there were any people in the world.

THE JOKE'S ON YOU!

How did the skunk call home?

With its smellular phone!

What do you call a grizzly with no teeth?

A gummy bear!

What do you get when you cross an owl and a skunk?

An owl that smells bad but doesn't give a hoot!

What do snakes do after they fight?

They hiss and make up!

What has hands, but never washes its face?

A clock!

What is a snail's favourite game?

Slide and seek!

What do you call it when an octopus gets its tentacles tangled up?

Scrambled legs!